MW01226783

**Good Words for *First the Spi***

After reading my friend, Tommy Hays' book 'First the Spirit' I found myself deeply encouraged. His explanations of the natural and spiritual man are very revelatory to anyone wanting to have a deeper life with God. I've heard it said many times, we are a spirit, we have a soul and we live in a body, but Tommy has a grasp on this concept that unlocks this mystery. For anyone wanting to walk a spirit-led life, Holy Spirit leading you Spirit to spirit, I strongly recommend, 'First the Spirit' by Tommy Hays.

Ed Sniadecki
Missionary,
Elder, Morningstar Fellowship Church, Fort Mill, SC
Author, *Overcoming Unbelief Trilogy*

I sat in a class with a large group of people in my own church. It's an odd place for me to be, being I am the senior pastor. I'm usually teaching a class, leading a study, speaking at a conference, or preaching our Sunday services, however by the middle of the class I wanted to stand up and shout because God released a beautiful revelation to me through Tommy's practical teaching. I have known Tommy Hays for years and my own family has benefitted first-hand from his personal, practical, and relational ministry.

What is beautiful about Tommy is that he never speaks in terms of theory or potential, but always from the vantage points of faith and real-world experience. Tommy has lived the words, principles, and truths you are about to read. He is both an eye witness and participant in the transformational power of God's word at work in the lives of thousands of people all over the world.

His joy is infectious. His confidence in God is unwavering. His passion for the Gospel is compelling. Get ready to embark on a journey of realigning your life according to God's heart. Challenges will be engaged, clarity will be gained, and your life's trajectory will be altered for today and for all eternity. Pace yourself as you read this work. Take time to underline, highlight, and take notes because you will want to return to these principles again and again.

Jimmy Pruitt
Lead Pastor
Bridge Church,
Fredericksburg, Texas

Letting go of our desire to determine our path, have our own destiny, and achieve our desired outcome can be daunting and challenging. But, surrendering to God's will is well worth the risk. The surrender leads us to a life filled with joy, comfort, and peace.

With honesty, clarity, and a passion for the Lord, Tommy Hays leads us on a journey to an understanding of the alignment between our spirit, soul, and body. When these are aligned correctly, our spirit can stay plugged into The Holy Spirit and keep our soul and body from directing our thinking and actions.

When Tommy Hays says this concept is revolutionary to many, he is telling the truth! It has realigned my thinking and taught me how to better keep my spirit, soul, and body in the correct order. This concept has enabled me to stay plugged in to the Holy Spirit and to acquire a powerful key that can unlock the door to the relationship with Christ that I so desire.

Cindy Jones
Author and Teacher,
San Antonio, Texas

# First the Spirit

## Right Alignment
## of Spirit, Soul, and Body

## Tommy Hays

### Pastoral Director and Founder
### Messiah Ministries

Messiah-Ministries.org

## Copyright Page

ISBN 9798747298361

# Table of Contents

# Introduction

I used to be a trial lawyer. I was representing my clients before the judge and the jury to achieve a verdict. Along the way, even though I loved what I was doing, I sensed a calling to lay that down and go into ministry. It took a while to lay it down; but there came a time when I said, "OK, Lord, I really do believe You're calling me into full-time ministry." So I went off to seminary to study for ministry, graduate, and be ordained. Little did I know, things would not be so simple and not quite as planned.

During the first year of school, my wife started talking about divorce. Ultimately, despite counseling and talking to my professors, my wife decided to seek a divorce. It was a time for me to struggle with shame, regret, guilt, the sense of failure, and thinking about what I had done that contributed to that decision. I began considering the questions, "Should I even go into the ministry now, or should I just go back to being a lawyer? Can I even be in ministry and can God even use me now?"

In the wrestling of all of that, the Lord made it clear that He will heal every heart if we'll just entrust our hearts to Him. He will forgive every sin we'll just give it over to Him.

He doesn't forget about us. He's right there with us, no matter whatever shame, brokenness, or trauma we may go through. It was during that time that I experienced inner healing and deliverance. It was a healing of my heart and freedom from the spiritual oppression that tried to weigh me down and take me out, seeking to defile my identity and destroy my destiny.

I experienced this healing and freedom for myself. As I did, I realized that God was bringing me to a place of deeper surrender and a new tenderness. And at the same time, He was giving me the deep desire to pray for this healing for others. In time, that became my ministry. It was just like God to take the place of my deepest pain and shame and turn it all around to a place of authority and calling in the way that only He can do. I didn't go off to pastor a church or become an evangelist, primarily. Instead, I discovered God was calling me to a healing prayer ministry. And that's what I've been doing ever sense—as best as I can and all by His grace.

My ministry of nearly twenty-five years now is especially in the area of inner healing, what I've come to call "healing from the inside out." It's creating a safe place where we can trust God to come into our hearts and minds, the ages and moments of our life, and to heal us where we're wounded and free us where we're bound. It's the heart of God to set us free from all that would hold us back from being all He created us to be. He did that in me. And He'll do that in you!

We live in a broken world that wounds our hearts. And who hasn't had a wounded heart along the journey of life? We battle a spiritual enemy who comes to steal and kill and destroy. And who hasn't experienced the intensity of the spiritual battles along the way? But the Good News is that Jesus is still healing the broken-hearted and setting the captives free! He still comes into the places of our wounds to heal us and our chains to free us! And then releases us to be all that God created us to be, even redeeming our deepest hurts into places of His great glory!

The same spiritual principles of healing and freedom in Christ are also principles of the Kingdom of God for growing up into spiritual maturity. They're principles for healing and freedom when freeing us from our past and they're principles for discipleship and maturity on our daily journey into the maturing into the image of Christ. I'm thankful to share what the Lord has shown me along the way, with so much more to learn every step of the way.

So come join me on this journey. Let this be more than a teaching. Let this be an experience, with powerful encounters with the living God all along the way!

Tommy Hays
Messiah Ministries

# CHAPTER 1

# Created Order: First the Spirit

First the spirit. Then the soul. Then the body.

There's a correct alignment of every dimension of our being that affects every dimension of our lives.

From a biblical perspective of our human nature, we are "spirit and soul and body" (1 Thessalonians 5:23). Understanding each part of our being and how each part is to relate to the other parts, according to God's created order and perfect plan for the peaceful, joyful fulfillment of our lives, is a strategic key of the kingdom of God that can revolutionize and revitalize our spiritual journey.

"May the God of peace Himself sanctify you entirely; and may your **spirit and soul and body** be kept sound and blameless at the coming of our Lord Jesus Christ. The One who calls you is faithful, and He will do this" (1 Thessalonians 5:23-24 NRSV, emphasis added).

Our human spirit should abide in deep communion with God's Holy Spirit. Then our human spirit—infused and led by the Holy Spirit—should direct the mind, will, and emotions of our human soul, which should manifest in the health and well-being of our human bodies.

All is well with my soul when all is well with my spirit. All is well with my body when all is well with my soul. But for all to be well, we must learn to allow the Holy Spirit to correctly align our spirit and soul and body: First the spirit. Then the soul. Then the body.

As we'll discover, looking more deeply into these three dimensions of our being, when we're correctly aligned with the human spirit first, we will live out our daily journey with more spiritual health and growing maturity, fulfilled with more peace and joy, walking in the wisdom of God instead of the ways of the world.

In right alignment, my human spirit, which is receiving my sense of guidance and discernment by abiding in communion with God's Holy Spirit, directs my soul. My soul is my mind, will, and emotions. So my spirit should direct my mind and how I think, my will and the choices I make, my emotions and how I sense and feel and experience the world around me. Then then my soul should direct my body.

In right alignment, my body manifests what's going on in my soul; my soul manifests what's going on in my spirit; and my spirit manifests what's going on in my abiding relationship with God's Holy Spirit. First the spirit. Then the soul. Then the body. This is what I call "Spiritual Alignment" or walking out my spiritual journey as a "Spiritual Christian."

But the trouble is that much of the time we tend to live out our daily lives in a different order than God's created order. Instead of living in right alignment, we're living out of alignment. First the soul, instead of first the spirit. First the soul. Then the spirit. Then the body. This is what I call "Soulish Alignment" or walking out my spiritual journey as a "Soulish Christian."

In that wrong order, when I'm out of proper alignment, I am more "soulish" than "spiritual" and all will not be well with my soul. In the "soulish" alignment, I'll be driven more by my own desires in the mind, will, and emotions of my soul rather than humbling myself to be led by God's Holy Spirit directing my human spirit. When I'm in a "soulish" alignment, my mind will insist on my own thoughts instead of yielding to God's thoughts. My human freewill will insist on my own will instead of yielding to God's will. And my emotions will insist on driving my actions by reacting from my soul instead of responding by the leading of my spirit being led by God's Holy Spirit.

Whether my spirit is "on top" and in charge, directing my soul, or whether my soul is "on top" and in charge, suppressing my spirit, makes all the difference. You'll soon see what I mean, as we unpack these concepts in more depth.

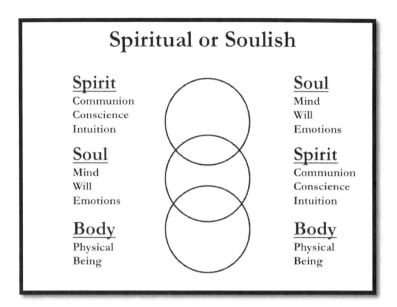

In this word picture, the three circles are aligned either in the order on the left side or in the order on the right side. On the left, the human spirit is "on top" and in charge. On the right, the human soul is "on top" and in charge. And as we'll see, alignment is everything.

The good news is that by the grace of God we can recognize it when we're being more "soulish" than "spiritual" and make a choice to humble our souls to come back into right alignment of spirit, soul, and body. By far, this has become one of the most revolutionary insights of my spiritual journey.[1]

---

[1] I'm so thankful for the teachings, writings, and ministries that have helped shape my understanding from so many wise forerunners, especially honoring

And as I've shared these principles of this book through the years, I've heard so many testimonies of these simple insights becoming life-changing for men and women at all stages of their spiritual journey to Christ-like maturity. That's why I'm thrilled to share them with you!

As I've taught these principles throughout nearly twenty-five years of ministry, using this concept of "the three circles," several have commented on how much this word picture reminds them of going to a chiropractor for an "alignment" of their back. When things are "out of alignment" it's hard to function and there's often a lot of pain and consequences. But it feels so good when things are "set right" and rightly aligned once again! We'll find the same is so true in our spiritual journey as well, as we understand the correct alignment of God's created order for our lives.

Someone has said, "We're not physical beings who have spiritual experiences. We're spiritual beings who have physical experiences." In that sense, where we place the emphasis makes all the difference.

Are we primarily physical beings who have a spirit? Or, are we spiritual beings who live in a body? Is there a difference between our spirit and our soul, and does it make

---

Rick Joyner, Watchman Nee, Paul Keith Davis, Francis Frangipane, Steve Shua, Mike and Becky Chaille, and Steve Seamands.

a difference? We'll dig deeply into these concepts with practical, everyday application in our spiritual lives.

I've found that for me and for so many others who have come to understand the concepts of this book, one of the most essential keys to living victoriously in Christ and advancing in the kingdom of God is understanding the depths of this relationship between our spirit and soul and body. While so much depends upon it, so little is understood about it. But by God's grace, we will now understand more and experience so much more of all we were created to be— secure in our true identity and fulfilling our God-given destiny!

In First the Spirit, you will discover:

How to experience God's presence more intimately

How to hear God's voice more clearly

How to yield to God's will more deeply

How to express God's gifts more powerfully

How to grow in God's character more maturely

How to experience God's pleasure more abundantly

All this, and so much more, is available to every one of us who learns to allow the Lord to rightly align us in spirit, soul, and body!

# CHAPTER 2

# Three Dimensions of Spirit, Soul, and Body

To understand the correct alignment of spirit, soul, body, let's first delve more deeply into the concepts behind each of these three dimensions of our being. Our foundational Scripture for this concept comes from 1 Thessalonians 5:23:

"May the God of peace Himself sanctify you entirely; and may your **spirit and soul and body** be kept sound and blameless at the coming of our Lord Jesus Christ" (1 Thessalonians 5:23 NRSV, emphasis added).

I like to graphically illustrate this key verse using the same "three circles" of spirit, soul, and body, but using ancient imagery often used to express the Holy Trinity. In the trinitarian or triune nature of God, there is one God, but He has revealed Himself to us in three different Dimensions, in three different Persons of His Being—God the Father, God the Son, and God the Holy Spirit.

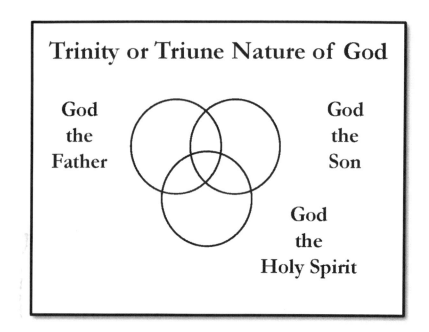

There are three aspects of God's Being, intimately interrelated in perfect agreement and unity, yet also having distinct identity. We call this "the Trinity." Though the term in not explicitly stated in the Bible, the revelation of this concept of God is very biblical, as shown in many contexts of Scripture revealing these three Dimensions or Persons of the One Being of God. A few Scripture references would include: Matthew 28:19; Luke 3:21, 22; Acts 2:32-26; Galatians 4:6; Titus 3:4–7; and 1 Peter 1:2.

You might say that that is one way we are created in the image of God (Genesis 1:26-27). There is one God, in three Persons of His Being. We are one person, but there are three dimensions of our being. We are trinitarian or triune in spirit, soul, and body (1 Thessalonians 5:23).

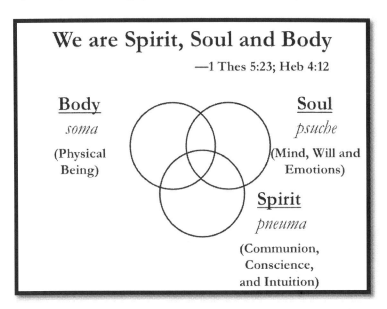

My diagram shows each part of our being as a separate circle, but they are interwoven because these three parts of our being are intimately and intricately connected. What affects one affects the others.

In the following chapters, we will break down the concepts of each of these dimensions of our being with an in-depth look at the meaning of each word to see why it makes such a difference in our daily spiritual walk. But it's important to see the full context of the foundational Scripture first. So we will now look at each verse of 1

Thessalonians 5:23 phrase by phase and concept by concept.

## "THE GOD OF PEACE"

Verse 23 begins with the declaration of blessing, "May the God of peace Himself sanctify you entirely." This is Paul's expectant prayer and word of blessing, by the inspiration of the Holy Spirit, for God's people. Moved by the Holy Spirit with the Father heart of God, he wants God's very best for the people the Lord has entrusted to his care. He wants them to know their God and to know His peace.

"The God of peace" is the God of shalom, the God of healing and harmony, freedom and wholeness, with all things in right order as they were created to be. He comes to bring His perfect peace, His shalom, to every area of our lives so that we are at peace with God, at peace with one another, and at peace within ourselves.

Ultimately, God is redeeming all creation into an eternal rest of an eternal shalom. He comes that we may know and experience the fullness of salvation, without measure. He comes that we may have life and have it abundantly (John 10:10).

"We know that the whole creation has been groaning in labor pains until now; and not only the creation, but we ourselves, who have the first fruits of the Spirit, groan inwardly while we wait for adoption, the redemption of our bodies" (Romans 8:22-23).

The God of peace is the God who sanctifies. He is a holy God, who desires a holy people. He says, "I am the Lord; I sanctify you" (Leviticus 20:8). He says, "I am faithful and I will do it" (see 1 Thessalonians 5:24 above). The God of peace wants to bring the fullness of His peace into every area of our lives and all of His creation. His sanctification brings His peace.

Our "Wonderful Counselor, Mighty God, Everlasting Father" is also our "Prince of Peace," as our Creator made manifest to His creation in the nature of our Messiah, Jesus the Christ (Isaiah 9:6; Matthew 16:16). As they say, "Know Jesus, know Peace; no Jesus, no peace."

## "Sanctify You Entirely"

We are "sanctified by the Spirit" of God (1 Peter 1:2). And the Holy Spirit of the Living God comes to sanctify us "entirely" (verse 23). Some versions say "wholly," or "completely," or "in every way." The idea is that God wants to make us whole and wholly His. He wants to make us whole and holy.

For the God of peace, wholeness is intimately related to holiness. Every dimension of our being is brought into alignment and harmony with every Dimension of His Being. Nothing is left out and nothing is held back. This is peace; this is shalom. This is His will according to His Word. "For this is the will of God, your sanctification" (1 Thessalonians 4:3).

The truth is, God is not willing to settle for anything less. That's what 1 Thessalonians 5:24 makes very clear: "The One who calls you is faithful, and He will do this." Notice, He "will" do this. Also notice, it's the God of peace "Himself" who will do this (v. 23).

We won't do it. We can't do it. Apart from Him, we can do nothing (John 15:5). But He will do it—if we let Him. His part is to work it out in us, and our part is to willingly choose to embrace Him and His process—the process of sanctification and healing that brings wholeness and holiness.

We'll also explore another aspect of this call to be "sanctified entirely" in a moment. There are different perspectives in the body of Christ about what this means, and when we may attain this level of holiness and sanctification. But for the moment, let's honestly acknowledge that from Scripture this is Paul's prayer and God's will to sanctify us entirely—to sanctify *all* of us, *every* part of us.

## "SOUND AND BLAMELESS"

We'll address the key phrase "your spirit and soul and body" in just a moment and in great depth, but the following phrase in verse 23 expresses God's desires to keep His people "sound and blameless". To be "sound" is to be healthy, healed, whole, and free. The alternate translation for "sound" in the NRSV is "complete." This wholeness includes our healing and deliverance—to have the fullness of our salvation. To be "blameless" is to be holy, forgiven, free from sin, cleansed from all unrighteousness, and restored in right relationship with God. The God of peace, who sanctifies us, desires His people to be both "sound and blameless"—to be both whole and holy.

Inner healing and deliverance, the journey of the Holy Spirit healing us and freeing us in the love of the Father, the name of Jesus, and the power of the Holy Spirit is the theme of my book Free to Be Like Jesus! — the Transforming Power of Inner Healing and Deliverance. Many of these principles are discussed there as well, as a foundation for understanding and experiencing the healing love of God through prayer ministry.

The main theme of this book, though, is more of the understanding of the correct alignment of spirit, soul, and body, than the detailed study of healing and freedom expressed in my more extensive book. But I believe this foundational understanding is truly a key to living out the healing and freedom we have in Christ.

## "AT THE COMING OF OUR LORD JESUS CHRIST"

Many believe these concepts about being sound and blameless, whole and free, sanctified entirely are expectations of our lives in heaven. Yes, we will experience all of that when we get to heaven when we die if we have Jesus in our hearts. Praise God!

But at the same time, that's not what this key verse of Scripture is talking about. 1 Thessalonians 5:23 is speaking of us being sanctified entirely in our spirit and soul and body, being sound and blameless "at the coming of our Lord Jesus Christ." In other words, there will be a people on this earth who are living into that *now*. There will be a people on this earth whose hearts are committed and directed to be sanctified entirely in spirit and soul and body, seeking to be sound and blameless, as best as we can and all by His grace, when Jesus returns for His bride. That's "at the coming of our Lord Jesus Christ."

The Father has sent His Holy Spirit to prepare a bride for His Son Jesus. Men are part of "the bride," just as women are part of the "many sons bringing brought to glory"—it's not a gender thing or sexual identity thing, but a spiritual thing, with prophetic imagery and spiritual language that applies to us all (Ephesians 5:25-27; Hebrews 2:10).

Through the transforming power of inner healing and deliverance, through the sanctification of spirit and soul and body, the Holy Spirit is preparing the way of the Lord in the hearts of God's people and in the earth today. Revelation 19:7 tells us there will come a day when "the marriage of the Lamb has come, and His bride has made herself ready."

One day Jesus will return to the earth at His second coming to fully establish His kingdom on earth as it is in heaven. The kingdom of God is where God is King. And Jesus is the King of Kings and the Lord of Lords (Revelation 19:16). So when He returns for His marriage supper of the Lamb, He's returning in glory; and He's returning for His glorious bride. But for the wedding supper, the bride must make herself ready.

His bride will be a remnant and expression of the body of Christ made up of His people who have come to Him for inner healing and deliverance, for a people who humbled themselves to be set free, filled up, and on fire! Set free from their past, filled up with the Holy Spirit, and on fire with a passion for Jesus!

We can make a choice, by God's grace, to let the Holy Spirit come and minister to us and prepare us to be that bride of Christ, holy and whole. We're making ourselves ready by agreeing with God. God has to do it. But God looks for us to embrace Him. God looks to us to be willing to humble ourselves and embrace His conviction and healing, letting him dig up the roots that bear bad fruit. He patiently waits for us to invite Him to lay the ax to the root and dig it up, so that He can cast into the fire all the chaff, leaving what is pure and holy remaining. This is how the bride is called to make herself ready (Revelation 19:7).

As God heals and delivers us in His process of sanctifying and maturing us into the image of Christ, He is preparing us to be the church He created us to be. Jesus is coming back for a holy bride who seeks Him with single-minded faith and whole-hearted devotion. Before He comes to receive His bride, the world will know that His bride has been in its midst—moving in the power of Christ because we are living in the nature of Christ. As Francis Frangipane has taught, we'll have the authority of the name of Jesus on our lips in our words and prayers and witness, while having the character of the nature of Jesus in our hearts.

As the body of Christ, filled with the Spirit of Christ, we are the temple of God on earth (1 Corinthians 3:16). The Lord has promised that the glory of the later temple will be greater than the glory of the former (Haggai 2:9). "Greater works than these" will He do in these last days than even in the days that Jesus walked the earth with His first disciples (John 14:12). God has saved His best wine for last (John 2:10).

These are the days of "the greater works" of God that He will do through His people as He has promised. And He seeks to have a people to whom He can entrust such great power—a people who will demonstrate both His power and His nature (2 Peter 1:4). Though the Lord can, and likely will, continue to use whomever He will, whenever He will, as instruments of His grace and power in the earth, He desires a holy people who will be His holy bride to display His nature and reveal His glory (Isaiah 60:1-3).

These will be a people who have humbled themselves before Him to receive the cleansing and freedom they need through healing and deliverance to be holy and whole— people who are emptied of themselves and filled with His Spirit. They will be prepared, empowered, crucified in the flesh, and sanctified in the Spirit.

One day Jesus will come in His glory in the skies, but at the same time, every day between this day and that day, Jesus wants to come in His glory in our hearts. One means of that grace is through the transforming power of inner healing and deliverance, as we allow the Holy Spirit to set us free to be like Jesus!

That's the heart of my book and broader perspective of inner healing and deliverance prayer ministry expressed in my book *Free to Be Like Jesus*. But I've come to understand all of that begins with our willingness to be rightly aligned in our spirit and soul and body—not just to experience healing and freedom, power and authority in the name of Jesus, but to also grow up into spiritual maturity in the nature of Jesus.

"Building up the body of Christ, until all of us come to the unity of the faith and of the knowledge of the Son of God, to maturity, to the measure of the full stature of Christ" (Ephesians 4:12-13).

## "YOUR SPIRIT AND SOUL AND BODY"

The second part of 1 Thessalonians 5:23 is the continuation of Paul's prayer and blessing, "and may your **spirit and soul and body** be kept sound and blameless at the coming of our Lord Jesus Christ." This is the explanation of what is meant by "entirely" when verse 23 speaks of God's desire to "sanctify you entirely." These are the three aspects of our being which make up the whole person. In the original language of this verse in Greek, these are three different words with three different meanings, referring to three different dimensions of our being. To be rightly aligned in God's created order, it's critical to understand each word and its context from Scripture.

The Greek words from the original language of this passage are **pneuma**, **psuche**, and **soma**, meaning **spirit**, **soul**, and **body**. The meaning of each separate word and concept is found and expressed in the context of each word in the various passages where they are found. In a moment, we'll look in some depth at each of these distinctions and see why our understanding makes a significant difference in both the process of spiritual maturity as well as the process of healing.

There is sometimes some confusion about this in the body of Christ. Often, people think of spirit and soul as being the same. In some scriptures, that is true, but in 1 Thessalonians 5:23, there are three specific words with different meanings. That makes a difference.

It makes a significant difference that is critical to understand. It makes a difference in our healing, spiritual freedom, and understanding of our spiritual maturity, growing up into Christ-like nature. I have shared this in different forms of the years of my ministry, and I never tire of seeing the excitement when "the lights go on" as these concepts become clear, relevant, and practical.

Some teach that human beings are really "bi-partite" (two-part) beings instead of "tri-partite" (three part) beings. Their understanding is that the spirit and soul are really the same thing—interchangeable words and concepts—in contrast to our body. They basically divide our spiritual nature from our physical nature, our invisible nature from our visible nature. This is actually a fairly common belief, and there are certain passages of Scripture that do use these two terms interchangeably this way. But significantly, that's not the case in this key passage of 1 Thessalonians 5:23.

Scripture makes an important distinction in this verse and elsewhere between the spirit and the soul, between the pneuma and the psuche. The original words translated "spirit" and "soul" in the Greek of the New Testament are not the same; and the original meanings are not the same. The contexts of the Scripture passages where these words are found define and express their meanings.

Hebrews 4:12, for example, makes this distinction very clear:

"Indeed, the word of God is living and active, sharper than any two-edged sword, piercing until it **divides soul from spirit**, joints from marrow; it is able to judge the thoughts and intentions of the heart" (emphasis added).

To "divide" in this context is to expose in order to examine and to set in order. The state of our spirit and soul and body needs to be examined and set in order in accordance with the living and the written Word of God.

This kind of "dividing" is not like taking a meat clever and dividing one piece of meat from another. It's more like the concept of dividing the Word of God—exposing it, examining it, seeking to understand it, and applying it. "Be diligent to present yourself approved to God, a worker who does not need to be ashamed, rightly dividing the Word of Truth" (2 Timothy 2:15).

Understanding this difference is extremely important in healing prayer ministry and in spiritual direction. I've come to believe it's profoundly significant both for receiving our healing and for growing in spiritual maturity. There is a "created order" and a "priority of authority" in the relationship of our spirit, soul, and body. Just as in the order of this Scripture, there is also an order in our lives: first the spirit; then the soul; and then the body. I'll thoroughly develop this important point after we define and understand each of these three components of our being in their biblical context.

# CHAPTER 3

# The Spirit

In the Greek language of the New Testament and specifically of our key Scripture of 1 Thessalonians 5:23, "spirit" is from the Greek word **pneuma**. We get the word pneumatic from it. For example, pneumatic tools are air tools. Air, breath, life, and spirit come from the word *pneuma*. It is the innermost part of our being. The *pneuma* is the spirit. Pneuma can speak of the human spirit, the Holy Spirit, or an angelic or demonic spirit.

The human spirit, the *pneuma*, is the innermost part of our being. It's the place of communion with God where His Spirit fellowships with our spirit. As the Psalm says, it's the place where "Deep calls to deep" (Psalm 42:7). It's the place of intimacy within our being that rises in our prayer and worship of God. "God is spirit, and those who worship Him must worship in spirit and truth" (John 4:24).

We are primarily spiritual beings living in physical bodies, created for a spiritual relationship with our spiritual God. Together with one another, we are the body of Christ, filled with the Spirit of Christ, living in relationship with God through Christ (1 Corinthians 3:16 and 6:15–20; Romans 12:1–8).

## —Outer Court, Inner Court, and Holy of Holies

A helpful illustration of the relationship and the significance of our spirit to our soul and our body is found in the pattern of the tabernacle. The book of Hebrews teaches how the pattern of the earthly tabernacle under the Old Covenant was but a shadow of spiritual reality (Hebrews 10:1). This pattern of the tabernacle speaks of the pathway of drawing near to God—from the outer court, to the inner court, to the holy of holies.

In a similar sense, this same pattern also speaks of the created order of our human nature. The body is the outer court. The soul is the inner court. The spirit is the holy of holies.

Our body is God's tabernacle among us, our temple dedicated to Him, while our heart is His home. "Do you not know that you are God's temple and that God's Spirit dwells within you? (1 Corinthians 3:16). "Your body is a temple of the Holy Spirit within you" (1 Corinthians 6:19). In the outer court of our body, we "present (our) bodies as a living sacrifice, holy and acceptable to God which is our spiritual act of worship" (Romans 12:1).

From the outer court of our body, we draw near to God, that He may draw near to us (James 4:8). In this imagery, on our way to the holy of holies of His deeply abiding Presence, we pass through the inner court of our soul. With the mind, will, and emotions of our soul, we are being "transformed by the renewing of our minds" (Romans 12:2). We're surrendering our will to His will (Galatians 2:20). We're humbling ourselves in His sight, that He may lift us up and draw us near into the intimacy of His embrace (James 4:10).

From the inner court we keep pressing in with both humility and faith, even boldly approaching the throne of God's grace in both the Spirit of the fear of the Lord and, at the same time, in deep intimacy with the Lord (Hebrews 4:6 and 12:28).

In the holy of holies of our human spirit, we behold the Presence of God. Here, we behold Him with "an unveiled face" as He changes us into His image "from glory to glory" (2 Corinthians 3:18). We abide in Him as He abides in us (John 15:5). "Anyone united to the Lord becomes one spirit with Him" (1 Corinthians 6:17).

Our human spirit is the holy of holies of the temple where the Ark of the Covenant of God's manifest Presence dwells within us—within the court of the body and beyond the veil of the soul. This is where Christ sits enthroned upon the mercy seat of our heart. "Christ *in you*, the hope of glory" (Colossians 1:27).

In a latter chapter, we'll return to the imagery of the tabernacle and temple when we see the right order of alignment of first the spirit, then the soul, then the body: First, the holy of holies in the place of authority within ourselves, yielding to the presence and guidance of the Holy Spirit. Then, the inner court of the soul, being directed by our human spirit abiding in communion with the Holy Spirit. Then finally, the outer court of the body, manifesting and revealing the proper alignment of what's taking place within the holy of holies and inner court of our human temple dedicated to our holy God.

## THREE ASPECTS OF THE SPIRIT

The Spiritual Man, by Watchman Nee, is one of the most profound books I've ever read. It's not quite as deep as the Bible, but pretty deep. I've been profoundly influenced by the depth of his understanding and breadth of his biblical research on all the places where the terms spirit, soul, and body are expressed in Scripture.

From his thorough study of the context of Scripture, Watchman Nee describes three aspects or functions of the human spirit, the *pneuma*, which are very helpful in making practical applicate to our daily spiritual journey. The human spirit is the innermost place of our being where we are to primarily experience the **communion**, the **conscience**, and the **intuition** of our relationship with God's Spirit. We'll now look at each of these three aspects of our human spirit to help understand why the spirit must be first in the priority of authority of our lives as a "spiritual" rather than "soulish" Christian.

### —Godly Communion

In our human spirit, we experience "the communion of the Holy Spirit" (2 Corinthians 13:13 NRSV). That is where we primarily have communion with God. Our experience and expression of the depths of our spiritual relationship with God mostly takes place in our human spirit. Our human spirit connects to His Holy Spirit—deep to Deep, heart to Heart, spirit to Spirit, in communion with God. In a way, our human spirit is like our spiritual umbilical cord.

"Communion" with God is the intimate fellowship of our trusting relationship with Him. "God is faithful; by Him you were called into the fellowship of His Son, Jesus Christ our Lord" (1 Corinthians 1:9). In our spirit, we become one with Christ in the unity of His Holy Spirit with our human spirit. "Anyone united to the Lord becomes one spirit with Him" (1 Corinthians 6:17).

It's *primarily* in our human spirit that we join with the Lord in the intimacy of worship and prayer. We worship the Lord "in spirit and truth" for "God is Spirit" (John 4:24). It's primarily from our spirit that we cry out to God in deep intercession, as "that very Spirit intercedes with sighs too deep for words" as God's Spirit "searches the heart" (Romans 8:27).

I say "primarily" to continually emphasize that our spirit and soul and body are interrelated and interwoven, though distinct in identity and function. We seek to always hold the tension between understanding the parts and understanding the whole, just as in trying to grasp the spiritual reality of both the parts and the whole of the Trinity, with the limitations of human minds and human language.

Through the abiding presence of God's Holy Spirit within our human spirit, we come to know Him. "This is the Spirit of Truth, whom the world cannot receive, because it neither sees Him nor knows Him. You know Him, because He abides with you, and He will be _in_ you" (John 14:1, emphasis added).

This knowing of God, taking place in the "knower" of our spirit, is something that takes place deep within our spirit, before it is confirmed in our thoughts. It's a knowing in our spirit, a knowing in our heart, before it is a knowing in our mind. The Holy Spirit is a Person of God and He comes to abide in us personally. Jesus Christ is our Good Shepherd and we know Him by His voice when we are abiding in union with His Spirit (John 10:3). The children of God "are led by the Spirit of God" (Romans 8:14).

We don't "know" with our minds "how to pray as we ought," so we that need the Holy Spirit to show us (Romans 8:26). In the same way, we are not able to connect with God to know Him and experience Him in the intimacy of relationship He's called us to without our human spirit abiding in communion with God's Holy Spirit, showing us to commune with God "as we ought." As we'll see, this is a major reason for the right alignment of first the spirit, then the soul, then the body.

## —Godly Conscience

Along with Godly communion, our human spirit is also to be primarily the place of our Godly conscience. Our sense of conscience primarily takes place in the spirit. In my spirit, deep down inside, is to be the primary source of my sense of right from wrong, true from false, good from evil.

My conscience, in communion with God, is to inform and direct my discernment. These matters of conscience are to be "spiritually discerned" (1 Corinthians 2:14).

"These things God has revealed to us through the Spirit; for the Spirit searches everything, even the depths of God. For what human being knows what is truly human except the human spirit that is within? So also no one comprehends what is truly God's except the Spirit of God. Now we have received not the spirit of the world, but the Spirit that is from God, so that we may understand the gifts bestowed on us by God" (1 Corinthians 2:10-12).

We've all said things like, "I have a check in my spirit" or "Something doesn't quite feel right down in my gut." These are ways we express this concept. We're trying to give words to what we feel in our sense of conscience. This is to come primarily from a conscience that flows from a human spirit abiding in communion with God's Holy Spirit.

"The human spirit is the lamp of the Lord, searching every inmost part" (Proverbs 20:27). The Holy Spirit speaks to our human spirit to quicken the discernment of our conscience (Romans 9:1). By the blood of Jesus, the Holy Spirit comes to "purify our conscience" to "worship the living God" (Hebrews 9:14).

In the song "Give a Little Whistle," Walt Disney's Jiminy Cricket sings about learning to be led by your conscience. "Let your conscience be your guide," he sings. This is the world recognizing a spiritual truth. We really do have a conscience—a sense of what is holy and unholy, what is true and false, what is right and wrong, what is good and evil.

And this sense of conscience is to take place *primarily* in our spirit. The sense we have "down in the gut" is really "down in the spirit." This is the place of godly discernment. "Those who are *spiritual* discern all things" (1 Corinthians 2:15). Our conscience discerns down in the depths of our human spirit by God's "Holy Spirit bearing witness with our spirit" (see Romans 8:16).

So, deep down inside of us is a sense of conscience. It is also the place of Godly intuition. We intuit or sense God's leading.

Romans 8 states, "The sons and daughters of God are led by the Spirit of God."

## —Godly Intuition

Along with Godly communion and Godly conscience, our human spirit is also to be the primarily the place of our sense of intuition. In our spirit, we are to intuit or sense God's leading for our lives. "For all who are *led* by the Spirit of God are children of God" (Romans 8:14).

The primary way God leads us is by his Holy Spirit abiding in communion with our human spirit in deep intimacy with God. By this intimacy, he directs us; and we intuit, or sense, the leading of God.

By the intuition of our human spirit in communion with God's Holy Spirit, the Lord fulfills His prophetic promise: "Your Teacher will not hide Himself any more, but your eyes shall see your Teacher. And when you turn to the right or when you turn to the left, your ears shall hear a word behind you, saying, 'This is the way; walk in it'" (Isaiah 30:20-21).

This is how the Lord leads us beside the still waters in His paths of righteousness (Psalm 23:2–3). We intuit the sense of His prompting by His Holy Spirit leading our human spirit. This is the nudging of the "still, small voice" (1 Kings 19:13 KJV). Our Lord Jesus says, "My sheep hear My voice. I know them, and they follow Me" (John 10:27).

We speak of "women's intuition." Once again, this is the world picking up on the reality of a spiritual truth. We're created to sense the truth, and the Truth is a Person (John 14:6)—a Person who wants to lead us into all truth by the leading of His Holy Spirit within us. "The Spirit of truth will come and guide you in all truth" (John 16:13).

We intuit the truth by the leading of the Holy Spirit speaking to our human spirit through the communion of prayer and the daily journey of faith. The more time we spend with Him, the more sensitive we are to recognize the sound and the leading of His voice from Spirit to spirit, Heart to heart, and Deep to deep.

The Godly intuition aspect of our human spirit is primarily a hearing and a knowing in our spirit, as we sense the leading and direction of the Lord. "Therefore, as the Holy Spirit says, 'Today, if you hear His voice, do not harden your hearts..."' (Hebrews 3:7–8). We are to hear in our human spirit and then respond in our human soul of our mind, will, and emotions, as God's Holy Spirit leads. As well see, this is another key reason we must be rightly aligned in spirit, soul, and body, with our spirit leading our soul. First the spirit. Then the soul.

# CHAPTER 4

# The Soul

Our key Scripture of 1 Thessalonians 5:23 refers to "spirit and soul and body." Just as in our translation of these words into English as different words, these words of the original language in Greek are also different words. Significantly, "soul" is a different word from "spirit" in both English and Greek. As we will see, this difference makes a profoundly significant difference in understanding the importance of right alignment between "soul" and "spirit" in our spiritual walk, as well in experiencing the fullness of our healing and freedom in Christ.

The word in Greek for soul is ***psuche.*** That is where we get the word psychology, the study of the mind. There is also where we get the expression some would use to "psyche someone out" by playing "mind games" and "getting in their head." What we try to do to one another in our flesh is also what the enemy of our souls would like to do to us.

When we look in the New Testament, we have to look at the word *psuche* in the context of the Scripture where it's used. The word "soul," from the Greek word *psuche*, is expressed in three different contexts in the Word of God. It's expressed in the contexts of **the mind, the will, and the emotions.**

## THREE ASPECTS OF THE SOUL

From the different contexts of Scripture, the realm of our soul is our mind—how we think; our will—how we make choices; and our emotions—how we sense and feel our surroundings. We'll now delve a little deeper into each of these three dimensions or aspects of our soul.

### —Our Mind

Our mind is the realm of our thoughts. This is our means of thinking about God, about ourselves, about the world around us. God wants to renew the thinking of our minds and conform our minds into the image of Christ. "Let the same mind be in you that was in Christ Jesus" (Philippians 2:5). By the Holy Spirit, the Apostle Paul says:

*Do not be conformed to this world, but be transformed by the renewing of your minds, so that you may discern what is the will of God—what is good and acceptable and perfect* (Romans 12:1–2).

The mind is where we are called to fight the battle "to take every thought captive to obey Christ" (2 Corinthians 10:5). As we begin to choose to agree with God, bringing our thoughts into submission to the mind and nature of Christ, we begin to quit agreeing with the world, the flesh, and the devil. Then we begin to know the peace and the power of God, as He changes the way we think about Him and everything else.

"And the peace of God, which surpasses all understanding, will guard your hearts and your minds in Christ Jesus" (Philippians 4:7).

"You keep him in perfect peace
whose mind is stayed on you,
because he trusts in you" (Isaiah 26:3).

Though the battle can be intense, we can choose, by God's grace, to "think on these things" that are holy, good, and true, rather what is unholy, evil, and false (Philippians 4:8). In the victory of our battles fought on the battlefield of the mind, we can begin to live into the fulfillment of the promise of God's Word, "We have the mind of Christ" (1 Corinthians 2:16). Instead of living with "stinkin' thinkin'" we start to live into "Jesus thinking." As we will see, a major part of that victory comes when we allow the Lord to rightly align the mind of our souls in submission to our spirits, which are in submission and in communion with God's Holy Spirit.

## —Our Will

Our human will is the means of our power to choose. We call it our "free will." Our free will is a gift of God that a true relationship of love requires. We can't truly love God or truly love one another without the freedom of will.

God is love and He created us in His image for a relationship of love. "Whoever does not love does not know God, for God is love" (1 John 4:8). To have true love, the real thing, it was necessary for God to give us the freedom to willingly choose to love Him or not, to accept Him or not, to reject Him or not, to worship Him or not, to obey Him or not.

If God were to reach down from Heaven and make us love him, is that really love? Or, if he were to reach down from Heaven and make us obey him, is that really obedience? Or, if he were to reach down from Heaven and make us worship him, is that true worship?

Without the freedom of will, we would just be robots choosing the choices we were conditioned to choose or forced to choose. Life would be a façade and our relationship with God would be a farce. So, at the pain of knowing all the wrong and painful choices we would make—affecting ourselves and one another throughout all the generations of humanity—God still chose to create us with the freedom of choice and the power of free will. Love could have it no other way and still be love; and "God *is* Love, and whoever abides in God abides in love, and God abides in him" (1 John 4:16).

God sets before us the choice of obedience and disobedience, life and death, blessing or curse, the power to choose good or choose evil, to choose His ways or our ways (Deuteronomy 30:15–20; Joshua 24:15; John 8:44; and Luke 11:28). We have His grace to help us, and we have His Spirit to lead us; but ultimately the choices are ours and our choices are real.

Just because God knows everything and sees everything does not mean God determines everything. He will never will evil. He will never will sin. Evil and sin are consequences of our choices and expression of our will, not His will.

There are consequences for our actions and spiritual principles that come to bear, but ultimately, we must choose our own path. God will not override the free will of His creation; because the moment He did, He would be removing the potential of a relationship of love. He will not ever do that because He cannot ever do that and still be Love, being true to His nature which never changes, and creating a people for a relationship of love in His nature of love.

As we know, there are significant differences of opinion among Bible-believing and Spiritually-committed Christians throughout the traditions of the Church on this point of the tension between the sovereignty of God and human free will. Both are true.

There's much misunderstanding of this tension between the sovereignty of God and the free will of man in the body of Christ. Yes, God is sovereign. Yes, He is in control. Yes, He is in charge. But at the same time, God, in His sovereignty, has created human beings based on his nature of love. To have a real relationship of love with him or anyone else, we have to have the freedom of will to love him or not.

The concept and expression of freedom of will takes place primarily in the soul. It comes out of a heart in tune with God, now making choices in freedom, hopefully in obedience to God. In my perspective of Scripture and experience in ministry, I believe this is a critical issue to understand that God, in His sovereignty, has chosen to create humans and spiritual beings with free will.

So instead of forcing our will, God redeems the effects of the choices of our will that we make and others make in our lives. This is one of the most important purposes of healing prayer ministry—the redemption of the effects of disobedient choices made by us and by others, in our lives and the lives of the generations before us, as we bring them to the foot of the Cross and under the Blood of Jesus. And as we'll see, the exercise this aspect of free will in the dimension of our soul in response to God's grace is a spiritual key to coming back into right alignment of spirit, soul, and body.

## —Our Emotions

God created us with emotions, how to feel and sense and experience the world around us. Emotions in and of themselves are not good or bad. Emotions are our emotions. God created us to feel and be fully alive to the world He created, yet experience by the leading of His Spirit and by the healing of His love when our emotions are damaged or distorted.

We're created in the image of God and the Word of God is full of expressions of the emotions of God. But our emotions can be distorted and damaged. And the emotions of our soul can become a driving force in our lives when we're out of alignment from God's created order.

God wants us to learn to be led by His Spirit, rather than driven by our emotions—to follow Him rather than the passions and desires of our flesh that have not yet been sanctified by the transforming power of God. The "passions of our flesh, following the desires of flesh" lead us to be "disobedient" rather than faithful to the leading of God's Spirit (Ephesians 2:1–7).

As we allow the Lord to bring our soul into submission to His Spirit, the emotions of fear, anger, shame, lust, greed, jealousy, strife—and all other emotions of the flesh—begin to be crucified with Christ. "Live by the Spirit, I say, and do not gratify the desires of the flesh" (Galatians 5:16).

Then our lives begin to bear less fruit of the flesh and more fruit of the Spirit (Galatians 5:19–23). Then we begin to live more by the Spirit than live by the flesh. "And those who belong to Christ Jesus have crucified the flesh with its passions and desires. If we live by the Spirit, let us also be guided by the Spirit" (Galatians 5:24–25).

What Scripture often refers to as "the flesh" is not the literal flesh of our human bodies. Rather, it is the unsanctified areas of our soul—the areas of our mind, will, and emotions that are not yet like Jesus. This is the "flesh" that must be "crucified with Christ," so that the life we live is no longer our own, but the life that is lived by the faith of the Son of God (Galatians 2:20).

God gave us emotions that we may be fully alive as He is alive. He doesn't want to destroy our emotions or suppress our emotions, but sanctify our emotions. And part of that is learning how to yield the emotions of our soul to the leading of our spirit, which is being led by the Spirit. First the spirit; then the soul; then the body.

# CHAPTER 5

# The Body

In our key Scripture of 1 Thessalonians 5:23, the last of the three dimensions of our being is our "body." The body is our physical being. The word in Greek for the "body" is **soma**.

This is the outward, visible part of us, as well as the inward sum of every organ, tissue, fiber, chemical substance, and cell. Our bodies provide the physical house of our spirit and soul, forming the mortal and "perishable" dimension of our being (1 Corinthians 15:53). We were created by God from the dust of the earth; and as He has said, "You are dust, and to dust you shall return" (Genesis 3:19).

God cares about our bodies and calls us to faithfully steward them as His instruments and vessels (Romans 6:12–13). Even though they are only dust, destined one day to return to dust, right now they are holding the treasure of God's very Presence by His Holy Spirit in these humble "earthen vessels" and "jars of clay" (2 Corinthians 4:7).

Yet, even so, we must allow God to continually bring us into His created order, redeemed by the blood of Jesus— first the spirit, then the soul, then the body. Our earthly bodies are the vessels into which God pours His Spirit to accomplish His purposes. But to over-emphasize the body at the expense of the spirit and soul is to be out of God's created order.

We are spiritual beings, we have a soul, and we live in a physical body. They are all three inner-related. What affects one area affects every area of our lives. Every area is necessary, but every area must be in right alignment for us to experience the fullness of the peace and joy we're created to know and witness in Christ.

In the interrelationship of my three circles, I'm trying to express that every dimension of our being is interrelated and affects one another. One way you might see this is that the brain is part of our body. It's an organ of our body. We have the physical brain, neurotransmitters, neurons, axons, nerves, and so forth.

At the same time, our physical brain also affects our soul. Our mind is part of our soul. And the thoughts and beliefs of the mind of our soul are very interrelated with the physical components of the brain of our body. Yet we also are to have the mind of Christ and be transformed by the renewing of our mind, which touches on the spiritual dimension of our being. So spirit, soul, and body are all interrelated; what affects one dimension affects every dimension.

Our earthly bodies are the vessels into which God pours His Spirit to accomplish His purposes. But to over-emphasize the body at the expense of the spirit and soul is to be out of God's created order, redeemed by the blood of Jesus—first the spirit, then the soul, then the body.

God cares about our mortal bodies, and at the same time, He cares about us having our bodies in proper alignment and right order. They have a purpose as long as we are on this earth. So, He desires to sanctify our bodies, along with our spirits and souls.

# CHAPTER 6

# Spiritual Alignment in Right Order

In these next chapters we'll dig deep into the concept of God's right order of "spirit and soul and body," what it looks like when we're out of order, why it makes such a difference, and how to get back into right order when we find ourselves out of alignment.

We're created and called to be "spiritual" Christians. We're "spiritual" rather than "soulish" when our soul willingly submits to the authority of our spirit, being led by the Holy Spirit. Then our human spirit is permitted by our soul to take the place of priority of authority. When we recognize this and allow this, we allow the Holy Spirit to retore us to God's "created order," which brings peace and order in our lives, rather than strife and spiritual conflict within ourselves.

As I expressed in my overview at the beginning, God created us in the order of 1 Thessalonians 5:23, in the right order and proper alignment of "spirit, soul, and body." First the spirit. Then the soul. Then the body.

So let's return to our diagram of "the three circles" with the alignment of the spirit "on top" and in charge on the left side, comparted with the soul "on top" and in charge on the right side.

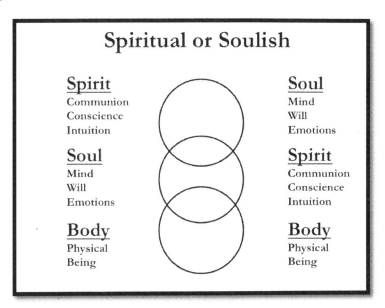

My human spirit should rise to "the top" to abide in deep communion with God's Holy Spirit. In the communion of worship and prayer, in the intimacy of surrender and trust, my human spirit can be infused and led by the Holy Spirit. Then my human spirit can direct the mind, will, and emotions my human soul. I can be filled with peace and joy, ready to respond instead of simply react to the world around me. Then my body can be at peace, at rest, on the right path of healing and freedom to live out my day and walk along my spiritual journey rightly aligned with God.

In right alignment, my human spirit which is receiving my sense of guidance and discernment by abiding in communion with God's Holy Spirit, directs my soul. My soul is my mind, will, and emotions. So my spirit should direct my mind and how I think, my will and the choices I make, my emotions and how I sense and feel and experience the world around me. Then my soul should direct my body.

In right alignment, my body manifests what's going on in my soul; and my soul manifests what's going on in my spirit; and my spirit manifests what's going on in my abiding relationship with God's Holy Spirit. First the spirit. Then then the soul. Then the body. This is what I call "Spiritual Alignment" instead of "Soulish Alignment" or walking out my spiritual journey as a "Spiritual Christian" instead of as a "Soulish Christian."

## GOD OF ORDER AND FREEDOM

God is the Creator, and creativity is at the heart of His very essence. He created us to express His creativity in ways that we have not even begun to imagine, much less live out in the fullness of our calling and destiny in the earth. Yet at the same time, **God is a God of order**. Even in the freedom and creativity of the expression of our spiritual gifts, He reminds us, "all things should be done decently and *in order*"—in *His* order (1 Corinthians 14:40).

God's order releases freedom and encourages the free flow of His Spirit within the bounds of His laws and His leading. His freedom and creativity is intended to move in His order, just as the banks of a river allow the river to flow beautifully and freely, without overflowing its banks and destroying the very lands and lives it's meant to bless.

As someone has said, "We need both God's law and God's grace. The banks of God's law allow the river of God's grace to flow." God's order is an expression of God's law, based upon His kingdom principles, which is always intended to be embraced with grace for our best and His glory.

God's freedom is a blessing, yet we can only receive the fullness of the blessing when we bring our lives into His order, by His grace. As Paul said in explaining the blessings of both freedom and order, "I say this for your own benefit, not to put any restraint upon you, but to promote good order and unhindered devotion to the Lord" (1 Corinthians 7:35). God does not desire to unnecessarily restrain us by His principles of order, but uses them to allow us to experience the blessings of unhindered devotion to Him with a fulfilling life on our spiritual journey with Him.

## ALL IS WELL WITH MY SOUL

As I said at the beginning, in this state or proper alignment, all is well with my soul when all is well with my spirit. All is well with my body when all is well with my soul. This is part of what the Scriptural promise means:

"Beloved, I pray that all may go well with you and that you may be in good health, just as it is well with your soul" (3 John 1:2 NRSV). "That you may prosper in all things and be in health, just as your soul prospers" (NKJV).

When my spirit rises to the "top" instead of being suppressed by my soul, I begin to experience a more practical application of some of these Scriptures:

"Humble yourselves in the sight of the Lord, and He will lift you up" (James 4:10).

"We lift up our hearts and hands to the God of heaven" (Lamentations 3:41).

"'Come up here, and I will show you what must take place after this.' At once I was in the spirit, and there in heaven stood a throne, with one seated on the throne!" (Revelation 4:1-2)

"But You, O Lord, are a shield for me,
My glory and the One who lifts up my head" (Psalm 3:3).

"Arise, shine; for your light has come,

and the glory of the Lord has risen upon you"

(Isaiah 60:1).

## THE GLORY OF THE LORD FILLS HIS TEMPLE IN US

In the days of Moses, the Lord specified in great detail the order for the earthly tabernacle that would welcome His presence in the midst of His people (Exodus 40:1–33). Moses set everything in order, and "did everything just as the Lord had commanded him" (Exodus 40:16). When everything was brought into God's created order, in line with God's commandments, "the glory of the Lord filled the tabernacle" (Exodus 40:34–35).

In Christ, we are the tent of meeting; we are the tabernacle of the presence of the glory of the Lord in the earth. As the body of Christ, filled with the Spirit of Christ, we are the temple of the Holy Spirit (1 Corinthians 3:16–17 and 6:19; Romans 8:9; Philippians 1:19).

And God desires to set His temple in order, to bring His people into His created order, redeemed by the blood of Jesus and filled with the Holy Spirit (Ephesians 5:15–20). Christ in us, the hope of glory—*His* glory arising and shining upon us and through us! (Colossians 1:27; Isaiah 60:1)

# CHAPTER 7

# Soulish Alignment Out of Right Order

As we've seen, all is in God's created order when we're living our spiritual journey, moment by moment, with our body is in submission to our soul, our soul is in submission to our spirit, and our spirit is in submission to God's Holy Spirit. In contrast, we're out of order when our soul rises up to force our spirit into submission and to resist against the leading of the Holy Spirit.  And we're also out of order when our body rises up to the place of priority, above the leading of the spirit and soul.

We're created to be spiritual Christians in spiritual alignment, not soulish Christians in soulish alignment. Paul speaks of the joy of life lived in the Spirit in the eighth chapter of Romans. But first, he describes the struggles of life lived in the dominion of the soul rather than the Spirit in the seventh chapter of Romans.

## INNER CONFLICT BETWEEN SPIRIT AND SOUL

Paul talks about a "war" that is taking place within the life of the believer (Romans 7:23), using his own struggle as an example. The unsanctified areas of the soul—"the flesh"— war against the areas of the soul that are yielded to the

Spirit of God—"the spirit." Peter speaks of this "war" of the soul as well, challenging us to "abstain from the desires of the flesh that wage war against the soul" (1 Peter 2:11).

Both Paul and Peter are speaking to Christian believers, those who already have welcomed Jesus into their hearts and have the Holy Spirit living in their lives. These believers have been washed by the blood of the Lamb; their names are written in the Book of Life; and they're going to heaven when they die. They are already experiencing a measure of the presence, power, gifts and fruit of the Holy Spirit in their lives; but at the same time, there is a "war" going on in their souls.

This "war" is an inner conflict between the nature of the spirit and the nature of the soul, that's giving in to the "flesh". Paul says, "For we know that the law is spiritual; but I am of the flesh, sold into slavery under sin" (Romans 7:14).

When Paul refers to "the flesh" he's not talking about our physical body of our physical being. Rather, he's talking about the human soul that rises up in self-will against the will and leading of the Lord, who desires to lead our human spirit by His Holy Spirit. I've come to define "the flesh" as "the unsanctified area of the soul." My book *Free to Be Like Jesus* addresses this inner battle in depth as a foundation for understanding our need for inner healing and deliverance, as well as growing up in spiritual maturity into Christlikeness.

## SOULISH CHRISTIANS GIVING IN TO THE "FLESH"

A "fleshly" or "carnal" Christian is a "soulish" Christian. This is our state when our soul takes the place of authority and forces the spirit to submit. In God's created order, there is a priority of authority where our soul should willingly submit to our spirit, as our spirit willingly submits to the leading of God's Holy Spirit. But we can also come out of God's created order and choose to allow our soul to rise up and dominate out spirit. Then we are "soulish" instead of "spiritual."

This is what I'm expressing by the alignment of the three circles as shown on the right side, with the soul "on top," in charge, and in control.

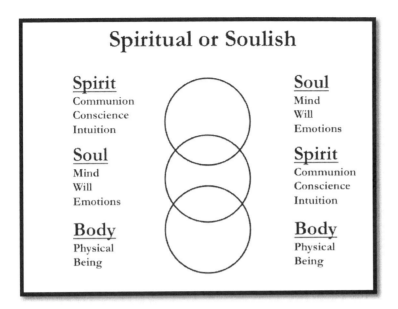

When the circles are aligned in the order shown on the left side, this represents a *Spiritual* Christian. The human spirit is sitting in the place of authority, in submission to the Holy Spirit. Then the soul is in submission to the spirit, and the body is in submission to the soul: first the spirit, then the soul, then the body. This person is restored and redeemed to created order—living in peace with God, peace with others, and peace within himself.

When the circles are aligned in the order shown on the right side, this represents a *Soulish* Christian. This person's life is out of order. The soul has risen up, has taken the place of priority of authority, and has pressed the spirit down into submission rather than being led by the Spirit of God. The soul is in rebellion when it is doing the directing and leading.

The *Soulish* Christian is someone who is being led by his own mind, will, and emotions; rather than by his human spirit in communion with God's Holy Spirit.

# CHAPTER 8

# Understanding the Soulish Nature

"Soulishness" produces varying degrees of strife rather than order; inner conflict instead of peace. The *spiritual* Christian is at peace with God, at peace with others, at peace within himself. But in contrast, the *Soulish* Christian is at war with God, at war with others, and at war within himself. He is not led by the Holy Spirit leading his human spirit; instead, he is driven by his own soul in rebellion to his human spirit and the Holy Spirit.

Our soul is our mind, will, and emotions. So our will is in the soul. We have free will. In our soul, we have the power to rise up and take the place of authority if we so choose. We all know times when we are "self-willed" and driven by our own will instead of God's. In our own minds, we think we know what is best. In our own will, we decide that we're going to do what we want to do, no matter what the Lord or anyone else wants us to do. In our emotions, we feel like doing what we want to do, when we want to do it, so we just do it. Likewise, in our emotions, when we don't feel like doing what we don't want to do, we just don't do it.

## MANIFESTATION OF PRIDE

All of this is "soulish." It's a manifestation of pride that says, "I'm going to do what I want to do." The soul is asserting authority and projecting its own will upon the spirit and body. When we're soulish, we're the one in charge and in control. We're being lord instead allowing Jesus to be Lord. We're leading the way instead allowing the Holy Spirit to lead the way.

This is submission to the law of sin because we are rising up in disobedience and rebellion to the leading of the Lord. The "flesh" is in rebellion against the "spirit" in this inner "war" of the soul (Romans 7:21–25).

## LIVING IN ROMANS 7 OR ROMANS 8?

The *Soulish* Christian spends much of his life in the inner war of Romans 7, but the *Spiritual* Christian spends much of his life in the inner peace of Romans 8. We can choose "life in the flesh" or "life in the spirit."

Just as the Holy Spirit does not force our human spirit to submit, our human spirit does not force our soul to submit. The soul has the power to choose because the "will" resides in the soul.

When our soul willingly submits, we begin to receive more of the mind of Christ, obey the will of God, and sense the world around us with emotions led by the Spirit. The Holy Spirit can lead our human spirit, which can lead our soul, which can lead our body. The communion and peace of intimacy and communion in right relationship with God in our spirit is then manifested in our soul and our body. We are restored into created order, redeemed by the blood of Jesus, and sanctified by the Holy Spirit.

The key to restoration in created order is submission to the Lordship of Christ, rather than asserting the lordship of self. One way is living by the law of the Spirit; the other is living by the law of the flesh. One way brings life, the other brings death. One way brings peace, the other brings war.

If we are willing to be really honest, most would have to admit that much of our Christian life is spent as *soulish* Christians. Rather than waiting on the Lord for the leading of His Spirit to guide and direct our human spirit in His ways, our soul rises up to take charge. At times we give our mind the place of authority rather than our spirit. At other times we give our will the place of authority rather than our spirit. Sometimes we give our emotions the place of authority rather than our spirit. We are out of order, in rebellion to the order of God, when we have the wrong priority of authority.

# CHAPTER 9

# Common Symptoms of "Soulish" Instead of "Spiritual" Nature

Too much of our lives in too much of the body of Christ is soulish, rather than spiritual. We suffer and the world suffers because of it. We're living our lives and following our own plans and agendas, rather than the Lord's. We're fulfilling our great ambition, rather than the Lord's great commission. We're building our own kingdoms rather than the kingdom of God.

Our minds are important, just like our wills and our emotions are important. But each has its place in God's created order. We must have all things in right order and right alignment to grow into spiritual maturity and wholeness. When things are out of order, we're stunted in our spiritual growth, conflicted in our spiritual peace, and confusing in our spiritual witness. Here are few examples:

## "SOULISH" MINISTRY

Much of our teaching, preaching, and ministry in the church is actually very soulish, rather than spiritual—driven by the **exaltation of the mind** rather than the spirit. We might even say, driven by the idolatry of the mind and intellect.

We often receive the knowledge in our heads, but not in our hearts. We receive it in our souls, but not our spirits. In created order, our minds are to confirm and understand what our *spirits* have received from the Lord. Not the other way around. Too much of our lives are *soul*-driven, rather than *spirit*-driven.

Yes, preachers, teachers, and leaders in ministry can be soulish. Have you ever been in a setting when the preacher is saved and is going to Heaven, but at the same time, there's a whole lot of intellect and education that's been given first place rather than the Spirit?

Even greatly anointed and Spirit-filled preachers and teachers can be soulish at times. I'm a preacher and teacher, but I admit I can slip into preaching and teaching and ministering out of my soul instead my spirit at times. That's often when I'm giving into the temptation and pressures of insecurity, pride, overly guarding my reputation, comparing myself with others, and giving in to the fear of rejection or false standards of success.

Yes, me too. "There is none righteous, no not one" (Romans 3:10). As it turns out, we're all on the journey to maturity, learning to die daily to our flesh and live by the Spirit (1 Corinthians 15:31).

We're called to seek the Lord and pursue Him. Not our words, but His. Not our ways, but His. Not even our prayers, but His (Romans 8:26). God wants us to get a fresh word from Him. He calls us to wait on Him to direct our minds for the people He has entrusted to us. He invites us to humble our soul, so that our human spirit can arise in communion with His Holy Spirit. Then we can hear His voice and sense His leading to preach and teach and minister in the Spirit instead the flesh, as a "spiritual" leader instead of a "soulish" leader.

## "SOULISH" WORSHIP

What about worship? Can even our worship of God become more soulish than spiritual? God created us to worship for an audience of One, for Him alone. Our spirit is to be caught up into the presence of God. God created us to worship Him in the spirit and in truth (John 4:24).

Even for a spiritual Christian, our worship can become soulish.

We may be thinking about the worship first. But then we may start thinking about the person in front of us; thinking, "Are they really worshipping or just drawing attention to themselves? Shouldn't they be lifting their hands or not lifting their hands; shouldn't they be dancing before the

Lord or not dancing before the Lord? Are they singing too loud or not singing loudly enough?"

Or we may start thinking about what everybody else is thinking about me; thinking: "What are they thinking about me? Do they think I'm really worshipping or just trying to get attention? Am I singing loud enough or not singing loud enough?"

Maybe you're too holy to have these kinds of thoughts, but I admit I've had them all at times! And instead of worshipping God as an audience of One, all my focus can get off of Him and onto myself or everybody else but Him in a moment when my soul rises up "on top" and suppresses my spirit. Then, I become more "soulish" than "spiritual;" and things are all out of alignment, stealing away my peace and joy and even my worship of God.

## "SOULISH" PRAYERS

What about our prayer life? The essence of prayer is really communion with God. It's not just asking God for things or begging God to do things that God doesn't give us and doesn't want to do. It's not learning the "right" way to pray with the "right" posture and the "right" words so that we'll be seen by God as good enough or deserving enough for Him to answer our prayers. No, the heart of prayer with God is really more of intimacy with God.

But even in our prayer life, we can be soulish. We can be driven in our prayer by our own desires, insisting on our own will, our own way, in our own time. The truth is, who hasn't prayed like that at times!

We can be driven by our emotions in prayer—driven by anger or hurt or desire for vengeance. We can be driven by greed, jealousy, envy, or pride. We can become so "familiar" with God that "familiarity breeds contempt" when we seek only the intimacy with the Lord but fail to honor and respect Him with the Spirit of the Fear of the Lord.

We can become so convinced that we know the will of God and the right timing of God that we can forget the heart of Jesus before the Lord, "Not My will but Thy will be done" (Luke 22:44). We can become so self-sufficient in our prayers or even prayer ministry that we forget to begin with the posture of humility before the Lord the Apostle Paul expressed for us all, "Likewise the Spirit helps us in our weakness; for we do not know how to pray as we ought, but that very Spirit intercedes with sighs too deep for words. And God, who searches the heart, knows what is the mind of the Spirit, because the Spirit intercedes for the saints according to the will of God" (Romans 8:26-27).

We can start off well in the Spirit but soon be praying in the flesh: "God, I am coming to you in prayer, but here's my opinion of what I think You should do or what they should be doing. And by the way, God, if You don't answer this prayer like You answered it for so-and-so in the Bible, then You're a liar, because You're not supposed to be any respecter of persons. So, I demand that You do this and do this now, just as I've said." That's a very dangerous prayer!

There's a humble and faith-filled way to remind God of the Promises of His Word. But there's also an arrogant, dishonoring, disrespectful way that insists upon the kindness and generosity of the Lord at the expense of remembering the fear of the Lord. There's a spiritual way and there's a soulish way.

Also, the Lord created us with emotions and even a hunger for spiritual encounters and experiences. But we can also become driven primarily by the desire for the emotional experience rather than the spiritual encounter. The warm fuzzy feeling can become our idol that we worship in the place of the only One who is worthy of our worship.

Something should happen when we encounter God. But when our primary focus becomes whether something happens or not, things are out of order. Then we're driven by the soul instead of the spirit; and the soul will suppress the spirit. Our spiritual life will suffer until we allow the Lord to realign our spirit, soul, and body in His created order.

We can even be driven in prayer by our emotions. We can think that we always need to have a warm, fuzzy feeling or the "holy goosebumps" or the "burning fire of the Lord" every time we experience a spiritual encounter in order for us to consider it a "real" encounter. God wants us to have amazing spiritual encounters, but when we are driven primarily by our need to feel it in our emotions, things are out of order. This will suppress our spiritual life. We will not have the pure spiritual encounters that we long for, because our soul is trying to be in charge.

When it gets out of order, we are driven by the soul, not the spirit. And that will affect everything—our mind, will, and emotions of our soul, our spiritual life, our physical body, our relationship with God and with others, and every dimension of our being.

# CHAPTER 10

# Humbling Ourselves
# So God Can Set Things Right

We can either be spiritual or soulish in our choices. And by our choices we live out the consequences in our lives, moment by moment on our daily journey.

The spiritual key to it all is our free will, the exercise of the choices we're free to make by the sovereignty of God from the "will" of our "soul." We can choose to be "spiritual" or "soulish"—with our spirit "on top" or our soul "on top" in the priority of authority of our lives.

God allows us the freedom to choose to rightly align our spirit, soul, and body with our human spirit rising up into communion and intimacy with His Holy Spirit. Then our spirit can rightly direct the mind and will and emotions of our soul.

But when we don't position ourselves for our spirit to arise and instead let our soul rise up to "the top" and be in charge in the priority of authority, we're more driven by our own mind and how we think, by our own will and the choices we would make apart from God, and by our own emotions that drive us instead letting the Holy Spirit lead us. Then, we're more "soulish" than "spiritual;" and all is not well with our soul, nor our spirit or body.

When we recognize our "soulish" state, it's time to humble ourself before the Lord and allow Him to restore us to the "spiritual" state He desires for us. He invites us to trust that He knows what's truly best for us to be fulfilled and free, full of joy and peace in Him.

## GOD REVEALS OUR NEED FOR REALIGNMENT

In the next section, we'll talk about practical ways to get back into right order with a spiritual readjustment and realignment that only God can do. But we have to let Him. He won't force us. But in His mercy and love for us, He will reveal to us where we're out of order, out of alignment, so He can set things right again.

The more we willingly choose to submit to the leading of the Spirit, the more our minds are transformed into the mind of Christ, the more our wills are conformed to the will of our Father, and the more our emotions are yielded to the sensitivities of the Holy Spirit:

"I appeal to you therefore, brothers and sisters, by the mercies of God, to present your bodies as a living sacrifice, holy and acceptable to God, which is your spiritual worship. Do not be conformed to this world, but be transformed by the renewing of your minds, so that you may discern what is the will of God—what is good and acceptable and perfect" (Romans 12:1–2).

In His mercy and love, God will show us when things are out of order.

He will show us what is going on in our soul, not to condemn us or shame us, but so we can yield our soul and let the spirit have authority.  It's a choice of surrender, of yielding to God.

And He gives us His grace to open our hearts before Him and allow His Spirit to search our hearts so He can set things right. As David prayed:

"Search me, O God, and know my heart; test me and know my thoughts. See if there is any wicked way in me, and lead me in the way everlasting" (Psalm 139:23-24).

## WE TAKE UP OUR CROSS TO DIE TO SELF

We can respond to the Lord's desire to set things right and put things back in His created order, redeemed by the blood of Jesus, as we willingly choose to allow Him to do it. He wants to restore right order, for "God (is) pleased to reconcile to Himself all things ... by making peace through the blood of His cross" (Colossians 1:20). But we have to let Him.

God's part is to set things right, but our part is to take up our cross by dying to our flesh and yielding our soul to our spirit to arise in right order with Him. As Jesus taught, "If anyone would come after Me, let him deny himself and take up his cross and follow Me" (Matthew 16:24).

It's a daily battle and a daily choice. As Paul said, "I die daily" (1 Corinthians 15:31). Moment by moment we choose to "live by the Spirit" by yielding our soul to our spirit, with our spirit yielding to God's Holy Spirit.

"Live by the Spirit, I say, and do not gratify the desires of the flesh. For what the flesh desires is opposed to the Spirit, and what the Spirit desires is opposed to the flesh; for these are opposed to each other.... Those who belong to Christ Jesus have crucified the flesh with its passions and desires. If we live by the Spirit, let us also be guided by the Spirit" (Galatians 5:16-25).

## THE KEY IS WILLINGLY CHOOSING TO HUMBLE OUR SOUL

Our will—our free will to choose God's will and God's ways or insist upon our will and our ways—is found in the soul, since the soul is the mind, *the will*, and the emotions. So the key to allowing God to set things right within us is what we freely choose with the free will of the soul we have.

Scripture teaches us this powerful, practical spiritual principle about humility and growing up to maturity:

"Humble yourselves in the sight of the Lord, and He will lift you up" (James 4:10).

Applying that principle to the alignment of our spirit, soul, and body, when we humble our soul, He will lift up our spirit. But the choice is ours to willingly choose to humble our soul or exalt our soul.

Less of me and more of Him. He increases and I decrease (John 3:30). That's humility and honoring His authority. And when we humble ourselves in His sight, He lifts us up to deeper intimacy and greater maturity.

We want to come to the place where we ask the Lord to put His thoughts in our minds and His desires in our hearts. Then our choices will align with His choices, and our ways will align with His ways.

Humility is one of the greatest keys to the kingdom of God. When we humble our souls, we let God set things right again.  First the spirit. Then soul. Then the body.

Our soul can assert its free will to choose to humble itself and let our spirit arise, so we are led by the Holy Spirit, abiding in communion with our human spirit. Or our soul can assert its free will to rise up to be in charge, suppressing the rightful place of our spirit, leading by our flesh instead of being led by the Spirit. Surrendering and yielding our soul to God restores our soul. Then once again, it is well with our soul—with spirit, soul, and body.

The Apostle Paul talks about this inner conflict and spiritual war going on within his own soul, between the spirit and the flesh, in Romans chapter 7. He says:

"We know that the law is spiritual; but I am of the flesh, sold into slavery under sin. I do not understand my own actions. For I do not do what I want, but I do the very thing I hate.... I can will what is right, but I cannot do it. For I do not do the good I want, but the evil I do not want is what I do.... For I delight in the law of God in my inmost self, but I see in my members another law at war with the law of my mind, making me captive to the law of sin that dwells in my members. Wretched man that I am! Who will rescue me from this body of death? Thanks be to God through Jesus Christ our Lord!" (Romans 7:14-25)

So even the Apostle Paul had a war going on within his soul. Even Paul had this battle about his will. But he was willing to acknowledge the battle and turn to the only One who could give him victory. When we turn to God from our "inmost self" of our spirit, humbling the will of our soul to Him, He will lift us up to rescue us and give us the victory in our spirit, soul, and body. "Thanks be to God through Jesus Christ our Lord!"

In gaining this victory, this is how Paul could pursue this prize of being dead to self and alive to Christ in his spirit, soul, and body:

"I have been crucified with Christ; it is no longer I who live, but Christ lives in me; and the life which I now live in the flesh I live by faith in the Son of God, who loved me and gave Himself for me" (Galatians 2:20).

Yet this was not a "once and done" but a daily battle and a life-long spiritual journey in his pursuit of the prize of becoming like Christ:

"Not that I have already obtained this or have already reached the goal; but I press on to make it my own, because Christ Jesus has made me His own. Beloved, I do not consider that I have made it my own; but this one thing I do: forgetting what lies behind and straining forward to what lies ahead, I press on toward the goal for the prize of the heavenly call of God in Christ Jesus. Let those of us then who are mature be of the same mind" (Philippians 3:12-15).

## HUMILITY WINS THE BATTLE OF THE SOUL.

I've learned along the way this practical definition of "humility" —to willingly choose to be desperately dependent upon God alone. This attitude, this perspective, is what helps me set my heart right before God. This state of mind and attitude of the heart is what helps me to humble my soul to yield to my spirit, as my spirit arises in worship and trusting faith in desperate dependence upon God alone.

So when my soul chooses to submit to my spirit, my soul is choosing to allow my spiritual life to take precedence, as I let the One who is Spirit take precedence over me. For "God is Spirit, and those who worship Him must worship in spirit and truth" (John 4:24).

## WE FIRST SEE GOD MORE CLEARLY TO TRUST HIM MORE DEEPLY

In order to surrender our will and yield to God's will, the Lord first allows us to see Him more clearly for who He is—to see Him "in truth" so I can "worship Him in spirit and truth." Then we can trust Him enough to surrender more to Him.

We can pray for "the eyes of (our) heart" to be opened and enlightened to see the Lord as He truly is. He gives us "a spirit of wisdom and revelation as (we) come to know Him" (Ephesians 1:17). We begin to see He loves us, He's for us, He wants the best for us, like a good, good Father.

It's not just an act of the will power of the soul, just out of sheer obedience; it's first trusting God enough to willingly surrender our will to Him, willingly surrendering and yielding to Him. We learn to trust Him more. Then, because we trust Him more, we want to yield more and surrender more to Him and His will.

# CHAPTER 11

# Some Practical Steps
# To Be Realigned in Right Order

Now we'll explore some specific, practical steps we can take to humble our souls and be realigned, no longer "soulish" but once again "spiritual" as we humbly allow God to set things right.

David said, "I humbled my soul with fasting" (Psalm 35:13). So as an example, there are spiritual disciplines, spiritual practices, spiritual steps we can take to humble our souls. When we humble our souls—whether through fasting or other spiritual means—we allow our spirits to arise again to the right place in God's created order.

## SOME SPIRITUAL DISCIPLINES THAT HELP US HUMBLE OUR SOUL

A few years ago, a lightbulb suddenly came on for me. The Lord began to show me this is much of what is happening in so many of the spiritual disciplines: contemplative prayer and fasting, experiencing the presence of the Lord in the Holy Communion of the Lord's Supper, true worship in spirit and truth, and even praying in the tongues of the Spirit. Everything started to make so much more sense!

With practical steps, these are powerful ways the Lord draws us nearer to Him, as we willingly choose to submit the mind, will, and emotions of our soul and the physical being of our body to the leading of our human spirit in communion with His Holy Spirit:

### —Contemplative Prayer

One of the beautiful outcomes of a deeper, more intimate prayer life is this reordering of our spirit, soul, and body. There are many different facets and forms of prayer. One of these is what many call contemplative prayer or centering prayer—the kind of prayer where we get still and quiet, to watch and wait for the leading of the Lord. At times we are called to "be still, and know that I am God" (Psalm 46:10); to "be still before the Lord and wait patiently for Him" (Psalm 37:7); and to come to the place where "I have calmed and quieted my soul" (Psalm 131:2).

This is a form of prayer in the silence of surrender. We surrender the desires of our soul to simply watch and wait in the stillness and silence of submission to God. In this form of prayer, we let the Holy Spirit center our thoughts on the Lord rather than on ourselves, our needs, or even our burdens for others. There is room for all of that, and the Lord often calls us to these other forms of prayer in petition, supplication, intercession, practicing the presence of the

Lord throughout the moment of our day and ordinary tasks of our lives, and even spiritual warfare. But contemplative prayer is a different form of prayer with a different purpose.

One of its purposes, I believe, is to bring us back into created order and intimacy in our relationship with God, and back into the communion of the Holy Spirit. Then this becomes the source of our passion to rise and go forth in the fullness of the power of God in all these other forms of prayer and ministry. When we get quiet and still before the Lord in contemplative prayer, we enter into His "rest."

The same Scripture of Hebrews 4:12 which speaks of "dividing soul from spirit" is actually in the context of entering into the divine place of "rest" the Lord has prepared for us (see Hebrews 4:1–12). When we enter in to this rest, through the quiet surrender of our soul, ceasing from our fleshly striving, the Lord brings us back into created order. Our body submits to our soul; our soul submits to our spirit; and our spirit submits to God's Holy Spirit.

Worry, stress, anxiety, and fear begin to fade away. Confusion begins to give way to clarity; and heaviness begins to give way to praise and peace. Then when we arise from the place of prayer, we arise to be led by the Spirit of God, rather than being driven by our own soul, or by the world, the flesh, and the devil.

This way, He restores our soul and leads us beside the still waters in His paths of righteousness, no matter what circumstances we face in the world around us (Psalm 23:1-6). This is a way He "restores my soul" by bringing my soul back into right alignment with my spirit and His Spirit (Psalm 23:3).

Then He's able to keep us at perfect peace again, because our hearts and mind are looking to Him, yielding to Him, and not trusting merely in ourselves (Isaiah 26:3). Once again, we're steady and secure in the peace that surpasses all understanding (Philippians 4:7). And we begin to know again the joy of the Lord as our strength (Nehemiah 8:10) and experience with a heart wholly devoted to Him that in the presence of the Lord there is fullness of joy (Psalm 16:11).

### —Fasting

The spiritual discipline of fasting is another means of grace the Lord uses to bring our lives back into created order. Fasting humbles our soul (Psalm 69:10).

The practice of prayer and fasting is not just some kind of Christian witchcraft to try to manipulate and control God into doing what we want. It's not just some form of "works righteousness" to earn favor with God. Instead, I've come to realize it's a powerful means of the Lord allowing us some practical steps to get our spiritual lives back into right alignment.

Through fasting, our soul and body are willingly choosing to submit to our spirit. This is why prayer and fasting go together; otherwise, fasting would just be a bad diet! During a fast, our body is hungering for food; yet we willingly choose to submit our physical hunger to our spiritual hunger.

Our soul wants to rise up in rebellion to the leading of the spirit in the call to sacrifice in obedience to the Lord. Our mind continually wants to think about eating and all we are sacrificing for no outward or obvious gain, trying to rationalize away our commitment to obedience. Our will wants to choose to eat and satisfy our desires, to assert its freedom to choose to forgo the challenge and test of our faith. Our emotions try to drive us to eat, in frustration and irritation, feeling all the sensations of hunger and sacrifice.

Yet, by the grace of God and the leading of His Spirit, we willingly choose to submit our desires to the desires of the Lord. This is a sacrifice of obedience, which brings joy to the Lord and peace to our lives. Our spirits rise up as our soul submits, and we are drawn more deeply into the intimacy of relationship with God. As we humble ourselves in the sight of the Lord, He lifts us up (James 4:10).

## —Holy Communion of the Lord's Supper

Receiving the sacrament of Holy Communion in the Lord's Supper is another means of grace for the Lord to bring our spirit, soul, and body back into created order. When we begin by confessing our sins and repenting from our own ways of thinking and living apart from God's ways, we are forgiven and cleansed of all unrighteousness by the blood of Christ (1 John 1:9).

Then, when we humble ourselves through repentance, the Lord then lifts us up into His presence, as we partake of the living Presence of the living Christ (1 Corinthians 11:23–26).

"The cup of blessing that we bless, is it not a sharing in the blood of Christ? The bread that we break, is it not a sharing in the body of Christ?" (1 Corinthians 10:16)

Whether we understand the Scriptures to speak of a literal reality, a spiritual reality, a time of memorial, or a combination, we can all agree that Jesus intended to use this sacrament as a means of drawing us nearer to Him in humility and faith. Redeemed into created order, we become "one with Christ, one with each other, and one in ministry to all the world."

In this means of God's grace, we experience the "communion of the Holy Spirit" through "the grace of our

Lord Jesus Christ" and "the love of God" (2 Corinthians 13:13). The humility of our confession and the obedience of our faith, as we receive the life of His body into our bodies and the life of His blood into our blood, bring our souls and bodies back into submission to our spirits. Proper alignment brings deeper intimacy.

## —True Worship in Spirit and Truth

Another means of the Lord's grace for restoring our spirit, soul, and body into God's created order is worship. In true worship, we bring every part of our being into focused adoration and praise of the Lord. Willingly, we allow our bodies to be living sacrifices and we worship the Lord with all our might "in spirit and truth" (John 4:23–24).

As "true worshipers," our mind and thoughts are actively directed to the Lord. Our will is engaged to choose to honor Him and love Him with all our heart, soul, mind, and strength. Our emotions are flooded with a sense of His Presence. And our spirits rise to soar into the heavenly realm of His Spirit. *Spiritual* worship, rather than *soulish* worship driven by our own mind, will, and emotions becomes another way of bringing our body and soul into submission to our spirit, so that our spirits rise into the intimacy of worship of our God.

### —Praying & Speaking in Tongues

The whole principle of tongues, praying in the spirit, used to be so confusing to me. But, one day, a light bulb came on!

Paul explained it. "I can pray with my mind, or I can pray with my spirit" (see 1 Corinthians 14:1-40). Here's a dimension of praying where I don't have to be in control. Instead, I humble my soul, and I pray with my spirit rather than with my mind. I can let the Holy Spirit pray through me. It's another way to pray to God in the right alignment of first the spirit, then the soul, then the body.

As it turns out, tongues is not just some weird spiritual experience that some weird Christians experience. It's so much more. It's a another means of God's grace to bring our human spirit back into intimacy with God's Holy Spirit.

The gift of praying or speaking in tongues is one of the biblical gifts of the Holy Spirit for the body of Christ. All of the gifts are given for the common good and for the building up of the body of Christ, to minister in the love of Christ, by the power of the Spirit of Christ with us (1 Corinthians 12:4–11).

According to the Word of God, there are "various kinds of tongues" (1 Corinthians 12:10, 28). One kind is when someone speaks in a language unknown to the person speaking in tongues, but is understood by others in their own language (Acts 2:1-13).

Another kind is when the Holy Spirit moves upon someone to speak out a message to the gathering of believers in a language of the Holy Spirit. When this gift is exercised, there needs to be an interpretation of the tongues so that the church body knows what the Lord is speaking and "so that the church may be built up" (1 Corinthians 14:5). "Therefore, one who speaks in a tongue should pray for the power to interpret," (1 Corinthians 14:13), or another person who has the gift of "interpretation of tongues" should declare what is said so that the prophetic word of the Lord is heard and can be obeyed (1 Corinthians 12:10).

"When you come together, each one has a hymn, a lesson, a revelation, a tongue, or an interpretation. Let all things be done for building up. If anyone speaks in a tongue, let there be only two or at most three, and each in turn; and let one interpret" (1 Corinthians 14:26–27).

But another kind of tongues is the personal prayer language of one who is praying in the Spirit. The purpose of this kind of tongues is not to share a prophetic word of the Lord with the body of believers, but to grow in spiritual maturity and intimacy with God.

"But you, beloved, build yourselves up on your most holy faith; pray in the Holy Spirit; keep yourselves in the love of God; look forward to the mercy of our Lord Jesus Christ that leads to eternal life" (Jude 20–21).

It's the nature of tongues, that we are not praying with the mind, but with the spirit—God's Holy Spirit is praying through our human spirit what is the will of God.

Paul says he can pray with his mind or he can pray with his spirit (1 Corinthians 14:10). He explains that when he's praying with his spirit, his mind (part of the mind, will, and emotions of the soul) is not productive because his spirit is now leading instead of his mind:

"For if I pray in a tongue, my spirit prays but my mind is unproductive" (1 Corinthians (14:14).

When we allow the Holy Spirit to pray through us God's Spirit prays through our spirit according to the will of God:

"Likewise the Spirit helps us in our weakness; for we do not know how to pray as we ought, but that very Spirit intercedes with sighs too deep for words. And God, who searches the heart, knows what is the mind of the Spirit, because the Spirit intercedes for the saints according to the will of God" (Romans 8:26–27).

In the gathering of believers where the Lord wants His message to be interpreted and understood, we need to pray in the spirit but with the mind also, so that the prophetic message is clear and understood. But in personal prayer, the Lord is building us up personally in spiritual maturity.

"For those who speak in a tongue do not speak to other people, but to God; for nobody understands them, since they are speaking mysteries of the Spirit....Those who speak in a tongue build up themselves" (1 Corinthians 12:2–4).

So, the gift of tongues has its place in the assembly of believers when there is interpretation; but it also has its place in the personal prayer life of the believer as a means of being personally built up in spiritual maturity. Paul spoke and prayed in tongues and wished that all of those under his care would speak and pray in tongues (1 Corinthians 12:5). Because of these blessings and more, Scripture specifically commands us, "Do not forbid speaking in tongues" (1 Corinthians 14:29).

## UNHINDERED DEVOTION TO THE LORD

In every area of our lives, we are called to "promote good order and unhindered devotion to the Lord" (1 Corinthians 7:35). These spiritual disciplines are a means of God's grace to help do that.

When the soul submits to the spirit, the hindrances to the flow of the Spirit of God through our lives are removed.

Then the life of God is free to be more fully manifested through our lives. We're once again at peace with God, with one another, and within ourselves. Then we can be secure in who we are and living into the destiny of all we're created to be. But such a strategic spiritual key to the kingdom of God for all this to happen is when we allow the Lord to set things right by restoring us to His right order: First the spirit. Then the soul. Then the body.

# CHAPTER 12

# My Prayer for You

Father, in the name of Jesus, by the leading and power of Your Holy Spirit, I pray for this one joining with me in the agreement of prayer. Take these words and Scriptures, these understandings of Your spiritual principles and begin to realign things in their lives, even right now, Lord.

Join me in this prayer right now, if you will. Say it out loud or say it in your heart:

*Father, in the name of Jesus, I am willing to see where I have things out of order in my life. You created me to have things in the right alignment: First the spirit. Then the soul. Then the body. It should be first my spirit connected with Your Spirit, where I have intimacy with You, where I have Your sense of conscience and leading. That should direct my soul—my mind, my will, and my emotions. My spiritual life is to direct my soul life—my mind and how I think, my will and the choices I make, my emotions of how I feel and sense the world around me. And that is direct my body.*

*So, Lord, show me where things are out of alignment in my heart. Show me where things out of alignment in my life. Maybe they're out of alignment in general, for this season, or even just for today? Maybe the lack of alignment is coming out of something I've experienced recently or maybe long ago in my life. Wherever it comes from, I give You permission to search my life, to search out my heart. Show me where things are out of alignment, out of order.*

Take a moment and let Him do that. He can show you places where your mind is in control....

Maybe you have given your mind, your thoughts, your education, or your intellect too much of a place of authority in your life, instead of taking those good things that God has given you and yielding them to His authority....

You may have insisted on your own way. Maybe not in all areas, but in some. You have said, "I am in charge. I'm in control. I'm going to insist on my own way, regardless of God's way or God's Word." Maybe you've said in your heart, "I'm going to protect myself. I'm going to put up a wall to guard myself. I don't need anybody or anything, just myself. And maybe you didn't realize it or consciously think it, but it's all been in your own power, your own wisdom, your own way instead of desperately depending upon God alone. Ask Him to show you, "Lord, is there someplace where I have been in control instead of You? ....

Is there a place or a time where you're allowing yourself to be driven by your emotions instead of being led by God's Spirit? Maybe there are times when you're driven by anger, shame, rejection, lust, fear, pride, greed, discouragement, depression, hopelessness or despair....

Whether it's in your mind, your will, or your emotions, allow the Holy Spirit to lead you to humble yourself, to humble your soul, so that He can cause your spirit to arise and be restored to right order.

After the Lord reveals these places of the soul that are out of order and right alignment, let's now pray for Him to set things right, as you willingly choose to humble your soul. Let Him forgive you and realign you.

Let's continue to pray, in humility and faith. Join with me in this prayer, if you will:

*Lord, forgive me for where I've come out of order and out of right alignment. Forgive me for when I've let my soul arise and suppressed my spirit. Forgive me for when I've asserted my own mind, my own will, my own emotions, above Your leading in my spirit.*

*For every place You've shown me, and all other places they represent, now and throughout the moments of my life, I repent and turn to You. Change my mind; change my heart. Forgive me and cleanse me from all unrighteousness and come set things right again.*

*Father, in the name of Jesus, I receive Your forgiveness and I receive Your grace to help me come back into right alignment. Forgiven and free, help me now see You as You truly are. Help me worship You in spirit and truth. Help me trust You more to entrust more of my life to You. May You increase and I decrease in yielding my will to Your will, my ways to Your ways. Begin to put Your thoughts in my mind and Your desires in my heart, lead me in the path of righteousness as You set things right within me.*

*As best as I can right now and all by the power of Your grace You supply, I willing choose to humble myself in Your sight. I bring my body into submission to my soul. I bring my soul into submission to my spirit. And I bring my spirit into submission to Your Holy Spirit.*

*Bring my human spirit back into deep communion with Your Holy Spirit. Let Your Spirit give me my sense of guidance and leading and discernment. Let Your Spirit embrace by spirit to direct my mind and how I think, my will and the choices I make, my emotions and how I sense and feel and experience the world around me. And may my body manifest what's going on now in my spirit and my soul, with You in complete control. I willingly choose to be desperately dependent upon You alone. I am Yours and You are mine.*

As you yield to God, He is forgiving you and releasing you. He is realigning you in spirit, soul, and body. He's drawing you near, to hear His voice and follow the leading of His Spirit. He's putting His thoughts in your mind and His desires in your heart. He's setting things right: First the spirit. Then the soul. Then the body.

And now you will begin to experience, even right now and in the days to come, more of His peace and joy in your daily journey with Him. All because He loves you and He's for you!

Even if you were to get out of alignment again, you'll be much more sensitive to His leading and receptive to His correction to come right back to this deep place of humility and trust for Him to set things right again.

Now let's just thank the Lord for all He has done and will continue to do!

*Praise You, Lord—Father, Son, and Holy Spirit of God! I thank You for all You have done and will continue to do! I worship You in spirit and truth. And I thank You with all my heart. Let my spirit and soul be free! Let my body be healed and whole! And let my life be Yours, a holy living sacrifice, wholly devoted to You. In Jesus' name I pray. Amen!*

God bless you!

"The Lord bless you and keep you;

The Lord make His face shine upon you,

And be gracious to you;

The Lord lift up His countenance upon you,

And give you peace" (Numbers 6:24-26 NKJV). Amen.

—Tommy Hays


If this book has been a blessing and encouragement to you from the Lord, we'd love to hear from you!

Tommy and Rocio Hays

Messiah Ministries | Messiah-Ministries.org

# About the Author

**Rev. Tommy Hays** is the Pastoral Director and Founder of Messiah Ministries. Called to ministry from a successful career as a trial lawyer, he is now ordained as an Elder in the United Methodist Church under special appointment as a spiritual director in healing and deliverance prayer ministry and member of the Fellowship of Ministries of MorningStar Ministries.

Tommy's degrees include a Master of Divinity from Asbury Theological Seminary, as well as a BBA and Doctor of Jurisprudence from The University of Texas at Austin. He serves on the Advisory Council of Aldersgate Renewal Ministries, on the and previously on the boards of Spiritual Leadership, Inc., the National Christian Foundation-Kentucky, Rapha God Ministries, and as an Area Advisor for Aglow International.

His daily prayer devotional, *Morning by Morning*, is followed by readers around the world each day and his book *Free to Be Like Jesus —Transforming Power of Inner Healing & Deliverance* is a standard resource for equipping and training in healing prayer ministry.

# Contact Information

## Ministry Resources and Speaking Engagements

Tommy & Rocio Hays
Messiah Ministries
412 S. Adams Street #148
Fredericksburg, Texas 78624
www.messiah-ministries.org
tommyhays@messiah-ministries.org

Other Spiritual Books by Tommy Hays:

*Free to Be Like Jesus—Transforming Power of Inner Healing & Deliverance*

*Morning by Morning—Prayer Journey with Tommy Hays, Original Edition and Second Edition*

Made in the USA
Middletown, DE
13 September 2023

38481380R00060